Properties of Matter

Flexibility

Arthur Best

Cavendish
Square
New York

Published in 2019 by Cavendish Square Publishing, LLC
243 5th Avenue, Suite 136, New York, NY 10016

Website: cavendishsq.com

This publication represents the opinions and views of the author based on his or her personal experience, knowledge, and research. The information in this book serves as a general guide only. The author and publisher have used their best efforts in preparing this book and disclaim liability rising directly or indirectly from the use and application of this book.

All websites were available and accurate when this book was sent to press.

Library of Congress Cataloging-in-Publication Data

Names: Best, B. J., 1976- author.
Title: Flexibility / Arthur Best.
Description: First edition. | New York : Cavendish Square, [2018] |
Series: Properties of matter | Audience: K to grade 3. | Includes index.
Identifiers: LCCN 2018013824 (print) | LCCN 2018016089 (ebook) |
ISBN 9781502641878 (ebook) | ISBN 9781502641861 (library bound) |
ISBN 9781502641847 (pbk.) | ISBN 9781502641854 (6 pack)
Subjects: LCSH: Matter--Properties--Juvenile literature. | Flexure--Juvenile literature.
Classification: LCC QC173.36 (ebook) | LCC QC173.36 .B47 2018 (print) | DDC 530.4--dc23
LC record available at https://lccn.loc.gov/2018013824

Editorial Director: David McNamara
Copy Editor: Nathan Heidelberger
Associate Art Director: Alan Sliwinski
Designer: Megan Metté
Production Coordinator: Karol Szymczuk
Photo Research: J8 Media

The photographs in this book are used by permission and through the courtesy of: Cover Linor/Shutterstock.com; p. 5 Chris Clinton/Photodisc/Thinkstock.com; p. 7 Happy Stock Photo/Shutterstock.com; p. 9 Flashpop/Digital Vision/Getty Images; p. 11 Julie Alissi/J8 Media; p. 13 Yellow Sarah/iStockphoto.com; p. 15 SEInnovation/iStock/Thinkstock.com; p. 17 Lucent Patrice/Oreida/Alamy Stock Photo; p. 19 Dusan Manic/iStockphoto.com; p. 21 Eric Raptosh Photography/Blend Images/Getty Images.

Printed in the United States of America

Contents

A thing is **flexible** if it can bend.

Some **solids** are flexible.

Some are not.

A hose is flexible.

5

Paper is flexible.

It is easy to bend.

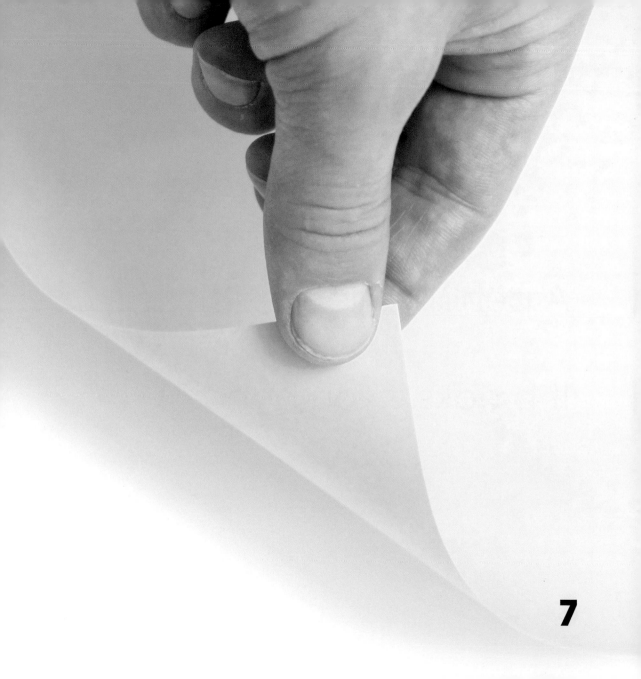

7

A pencil is not flexible.

It breaks if you bend it!

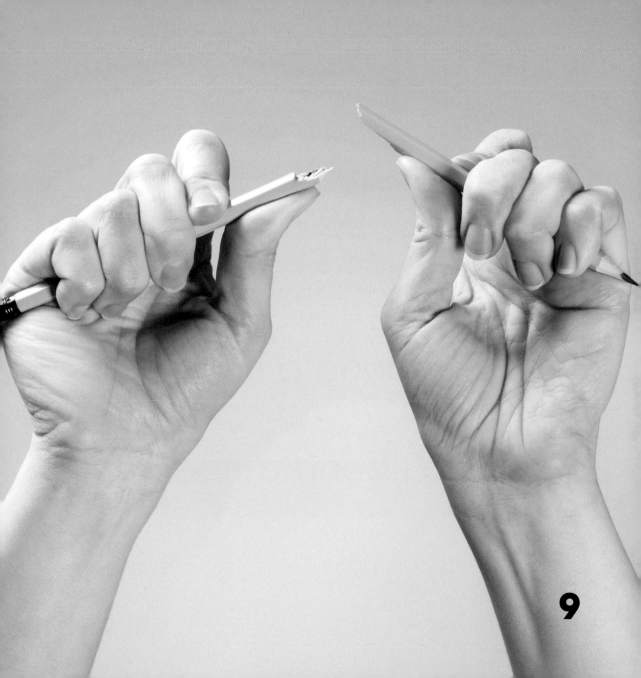

9

Thin things bend more than thick ones.

You can bend a twig.

You can't bend a tree trunk.

Some **matter** is flexible.

Rubber bends.

The bottom of a shoe is made of rubber.

It can bend!

13

Glass is not flexible.

It does not bend.

It breaks instead.

15

People have flexible parts.

Skin can bend.

Muscles can bend.

17

Teeth are not flexible.

They need to be **stiff**.

They need to chew.

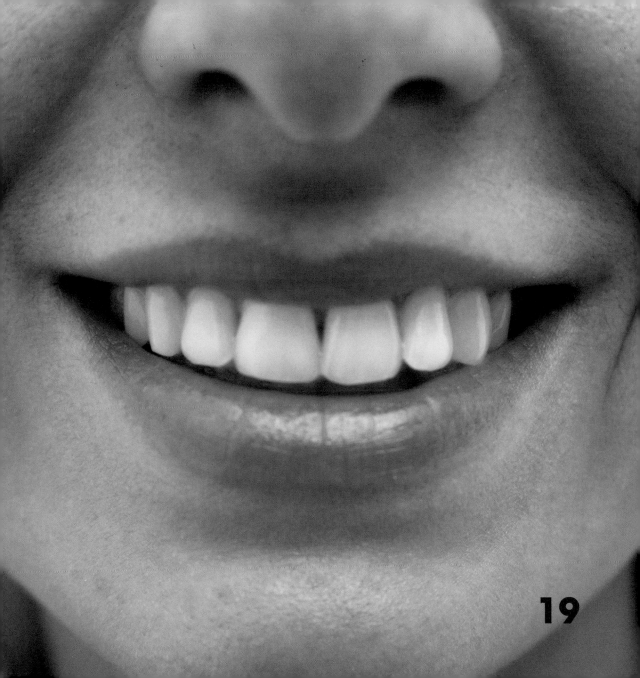

19

Many things are flexible.

A plastic bag bends.

A rubber band bends.

They bend so they
don't break!

New Words

flexible (FLEK-sih-bul) Able to bend.

matter (MAT-er) What objects are made of.

muscles (MUS-ulz) Parts of a body that help it move.

solids (SOL-ids) Things that are not liquid or gas.

stiff (STIF) Strong and not able to bend.

Index

23

About the Author

Arthur Best lives in Wisconsin with his wife and son. He has written many other books for children. He can be flexible.

About BOOKWORMS

Bookworms help independent readers gain reading confidence through high-frequency words, simple sentences, and strong picture/text support. Each book explores a concept that helps children relate what they read to the world they live in.